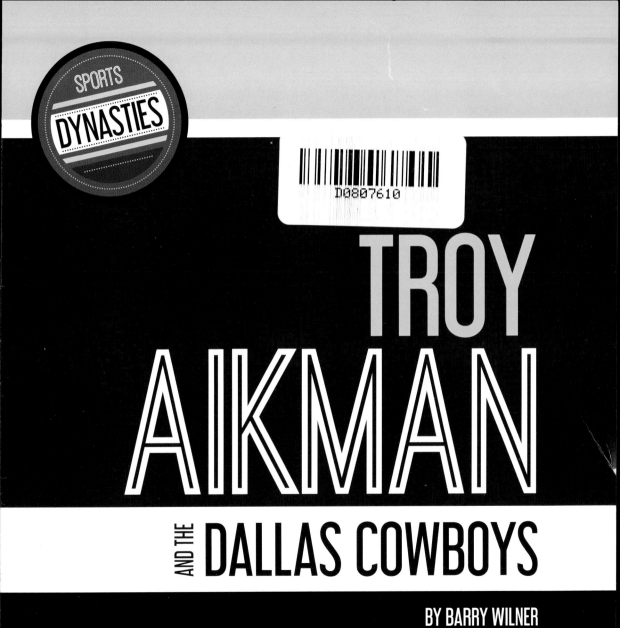

TROY
AIKMAN

AND THE DALLAS COWBOYS

BY BARRY WILNER

abdopublishing.com

Published by Abdo Publishing, a division of ABDO, PO Box 398166, Minneapolis, Minnesota 55439. Copyright © 2019 by Abdo Consulting Group, Inc. International copyrights reserved in all countries. No part of this book may be reproduced in any form without written permission from the publisher. SportsZone™ is a trademark and logo of Abdo Publishing.

Printed in the United States of America, North Mankato, Minnesota
042018
092018

THIS BOOK CONTAINS
RECYCLED MATERIALS

Distributed in paperback by North Star Editions, Inc.

Cover Photos: Al Messerschmidt/AP Images, foreground; NFL Photos/AP Images, background
Interior Photos: Paul Jasienski/AP Images, 4–5; Patrick Murphy-Racey/Sports Illustrated/Getty Images, 6; Tom DiPace/AP Images, 8, 41; Kevin Terrell/AP Images, 10; Al Bello/Allsport/Getty Images Sport/Getty Images, 12; Vernon Biever/AP Images, 14–15, 17, 18; AP Images, 20; Ron Heflin/AP Images, 23; Focus on Sport/Getty Images, 24–25; Eric Gay/AP Images, 26; NFL Photos/AP Images, 29; James Smith/Getty Images Sport/Getty Images, 30; Paul Spinelli/AP Images, 32–33; Linda Kaye/AP Images, 34; Susan Ragan/ AP Images, 37; Tony Tomsic/AP Images, 38–39; Katherine Welles/Shutterstock Images, 43

Editor: Bradley Cole
Series Designer: Craig Hinton

Library of Congress Control Number: 2017962583

Publisher's Cataloging-in-Publication Data

Names: Wilner, Barry, author.
Title: Troy Aikman and the Dallas Cowboys / by Barry Wilner.
Description: Minneapolis, Minnesota : Abdo Publishing, 2019. | Series: Sports dynasties | Includes online resources and index.
Identifiers: ISBN 9781532114380 (lib.bdg.) | ISBN 9781641852876 (pbk) | ISBN 9781532154218 (ebook)
Subjects: LCSH: Aikman, Troy, 1966---Juvenile literature. | Football players--United States--Biography-- Juvenile literature. | Football--Juvenile literature. | Dallas Cowboys (Football team)--Juvenile literature.
Classification: DDC 796.332092 [B]--dc23

TABLE OF
CONTENTS

CHAPTER 1

THREE
OUT OF FOUR

After winning the National Football League (NFL) titles for the 1992 and 1993 seasons, the Dallas Cowboys were in a great position to become the first team to win three straight Super Bowls. They were young. They had superstars such as quarterback Troy Aikman and running back Emmitt Smith. They weren't bothered by the pressure that came with being in big games. Then head coach Jimmy Johnson left the team.

4

Together coach Jimmy Johnson and quarterback Troy Aikman led the Cowboys to the playoffs in the 1992 and 1993 seasons.

Troy Aikman throws a pass in practice.

Johnson had been instrumental in the Cowboys' resurgence.
The Cowboys hadn't won a playoff game in seven years before
Johnson. He had built the current roster by drafting great
players and finding them in free agency. They won just one

game in 1989, Johnson's first year in Dallas. Two years later the Cowboys were in the playoffs. The next season they won the Super Bowl for the first time in 15 years. Then they won it again the following year. He would be a tough act to follow.

Cowboys owner Jerry Jones replaced him with another successful former college coach, Barry Switzer. But Dallas fell to the San Francisco 49ers in the 1994 National Football Conference (NFC) Championship Game. The 49ers went on to rout the San Diego Chargers in the Super Bowl. All the Cowboys could do was watch.

"When I'm 60 and I tell my grandchildren about this team," star receiver Michael Irvin said, "I will tell them with pride about a team that just kept bouncing back. But let me tell you this, losing's rough."

So the Cowboys made sure they wouldn't lose the next year. They set a new goal: No team had won three Super Bowls in four seasons. They would do that. To get that third ring, though, they needed to overcome losing some key players in free agency. They also had to overcome losing twice to their most-hated rival, the Washington Redskins, and once to the 49ers.

Troy Aikman takes a snap under center during Super Bowl XXX.

STARTING A DYNASTY

They did, finishing with a 12–4 record behind another strong season by "the Triplets," Aikman, Smith, and Irvin. They had the best record in their conference, and that meant their playoff games would be at home too. First the Cowboys made easy work of the Philadelphia Eagles with Aikman completing 17 of 24 passes for 253 yards. Then Smith scored three rushing touchdowns, and Aikman completed two more to Irvin as they beat the Green Bay Packers 38–27 to earn a trip to Tempe, Arizona, for another Super Bowl. They weren't going to let this one slip away.

The American Football Conference (AFC) champion Pittsburgh Steelers, who were 4–0 in Super Bowls, were playing for the Lombardi Trophy for the first time since 1980. Their rugged, run-stopping defense was joined by the AFC's top-scoring offense, led by quarterback Neil O'Donnell.

Having already faced elite quarterbacks such as San Francisco's Steve Young and Green Bay's Brett Favre during the season, the Cowboys were ready. Besides, they had the NFC's second-ranked scoring defense. A stingy bunch, the defense featured three Pro Bowlers.

Quickly the Cowboys took charge. They grabbed a 13–0 lead before the Steelers knew what hit them. Chris Boniol made two field goals, and Aikman connected with his other favorite target, tight end Jay Novacek, for a 3-yard touchdown.

Sun Devil Stadium was pretty much filled with folks in Cowboys gear. It sure looked as if there was no stopping America's Team.

But the Steelers' wide receiver Yancey Thigpen caught a touchdown pass to cut the Cowboys' lead to 13–7. On defense Pittsburgh kept stopping Smith's rushes. When the teams headed into the locker rooms for halftime, Pittsburgh had the momentum.

The Steelers didn't really want any part of challenging Deion Sanders, the NFL's top cornerback. Instead, in the second half, they focused on beating cornerback Larry Brown on the other side of the field. Midway through the third quarter, that idea backfired. Brown picked off O'Donnell's pass and returned it 44 yards to the Steelers' 18-yard line. Soon Smith plunged in from a yard out to make it 20–7.

FINISHING STRONG

Back came Pittsburgh once more, but the Steelers were held to a field goal. The Cowboys were looking good with a 10-point lead. Then, to everyone's surprise, Pittsburgh attempted an onside kick. When the Steelers recovered it, they marched down

the field. Bam Morris crashed in from one yard out to make it 20–17. After a Dallas punt, Pittsburgh had a chance to spoil the party for all those folks wearing the silver star.

Brown came to the rescue again. He intercepted O'Donnell's pass and ran it back 33 yards. Smith converted the turnover into a touchdown again, and the championship belonged to Dallas. Soon after, the Cowboys and their fans were jumping for joy. Dallas had won three Super Bowls in four years.

RIVALS AND REPLACEMENTS

Jimmy Johnson and Jerry Jones had been teammates at the University of Arkansas. But when Johnson left the Dallas Cowboys over a dispute with his friend and former teammate, Jones hired Barry Switzer. Johnson and Switzer had been bitter rivals when Johnson coached Oklahoma State and Switzer was in charge at Oklahoma.

CHAPTER 2

THE
LANDRY YEARS

Before their dynasty of the 1990s, the Dallas Cowboys had a mini-dynasty. They won two Super Bowls under coach Tom Landry. They went to three others, becoming the first team to reach five Super Bowls. Dallas also fell one step short of the big game seven times with Landry as coach, all between 1966 and 1982.

In many ways, the Cowboys changed how NFL teams were run. They were one of the first clubs in any major sport to use computers.

Cowboys defensive back Cornell Green talks with coach Tom Landry during Super Bowl VI, in 1972.

Thanks to general manager Tex Schramm and personnel director Gil Brandt, they scouted small schools and historically black colleges before other teams did. Such great Cowboys as receiver Bob Hayes, defensive linemen Jethro Pugh, and defensive end Ed "Too Tall" Jones came from those schools.

However, the early years of Cowboys football had some growing pains. The team had begun play in 1960. That was the same year another local team, the Dallas Texans, begun play in the American Football League (AFL). In those years, the Texans were the more successful team. They even won the 1962 AFL championship. The Cowboys, meanwhile, started 9–28–3. As the 1960s went on though, things began to change.

In 1963 the Texans moved to Kansas City and became the Chiefs. They believed the Cowboys would always be more popular in Dallas. They were right. In fact by 1979 the Cowboys were regularly called "America's Team" by fans and the media.

It took until 1966 for the Cowboys to make the playoffs. The NFL's top team at the time was the Green Bay Packers. Legendary head coach Vince Lombardi brought his team of future Hall of Famers to the Cotton Bowl on New Year's Day to play for the league's title. The Cowboys took the Packers

In 1967 Dallas traveled to Green Bay to play what would be known as the Ice Bowl.

down to the final seconds. But trailing 34–27, quarterback

Don Meredith's short pass into the end zone was picked off by

Green Bay safety Tom Brown, and the Packers won.

The next week, Green Bay won the first Super Bowl as the Cowboys waited for another chance. That chance came the very next season. This time, on December 31, 1967, they traveled to frigid Green Bay. The temperature at game time was minus-13 degrees Fahrenheit (−25°C). The wind chill was minus-40 (−40° C). Much of the Lambeau Field turf was frozen.

THE ICE BOWL

When referee Norm Schacter blew his whistle to start the game, it froze to his lips. "I thought when it got to 32 degrees (0°C) and ice froze, you couldn't get any colder," Dallas halfback Dan Reeves said. "But you can feel every degree of it."

Still, they played, and more than 50,000 fans showed up for the "Ice Bowl." They cheered as loudly as they could through their ski masks when the Packers went ahead 14–0. But the Cowboys came back. On the opening play of the fourth quarter, Reeves took a pitch from quarterback Don Meredith. The defense all moved toward Reeves. Then he surprised the Packers defense by passing to wide receiver Lance Rentzel. The 50-yard touchdown gave Dallas a 17–14 lead.

Roger Staubach throws a pass during Dallas's 1971 championship season.

The great Packers weren't through though. Hall of Fame
quarterback Bart Starr marched them downfield in the
final minutes. They got inside the Dallas 1-yard line with only

16 seconds remaining and no timeouts left. They could have kicked a field goal to force overtime, but no one wanted to stay out there any longer. So with the most famous quarterback sneak in football history, Starr and the Packers prevailed. Again Cowboys hearts were broken. When would a championship come?

GETTING CLOSE

Not in 1970, when Dallas made its first Super Bowl and again lost in the final seconds, this time on Baltimore Colts kicker Jim O'Brien's field goal. But the next year, future Hall of Fame quarterback Roger Staubach took over, and the Cowboys put together a great defense. Veteran defensive tackle Bob Lilly anchored the line, and cornerback Herb Adderley, who played for those great Packers teams in the 1960s, provided leadership on the back end. With the pieces in place, the Cowboys won their first Super Bowl, beating the Miami Dolphins 24–3.

Dallas won the NFL crown in 1977 too, beating Denver 27–10. Landry's Cowboys also lost two Super Bowls to the Steelers, after the 1975 and 1978 seasons. The Cowboys were back in the NFC Championship Game in 1980, 1981, and 1982, but lost all three. Over a 17-year span, Dallas went to 12 conference championship games and won five of them.

The Cowboys had become so popular that in 1982 they had more games on *Monday Night Football* than anyone else. Even when they stopped making it to the big games, their fans still loved them. Their early dynasty had come to an end, but America still watched their games. But when they had three straight losing records and the team was sold to Jerry Jones in 1989, big changes were coming.

HALL OF FAMERS

Along with president Tex Schramm and head coach Tom Landry, seven players from the earlier dynasty were inducted into the Pro Football Hall of Fame as Cowboys: running back Tony Dorsett, wide receiver Bob Hayes, defensive tackle Bob Lilly, cornerback Mel Renfro, quarterback Roger Staubach, defensive tackle Randy White, and offensive tackle Rayfield Wright. Other Hall members who played for Dallas in that time period were cornerback Herb Adderley, wide receiver Lance Alworth, tight end Mike Ditka, offensive tackle Forrest Gregg, wide receiver Tommy McDonald, and tight end Jackie Smith.

CHAPTER 3

KEY FIGURES

America's Team was struggling, but that didn't deter Jerry Jones, a Texas oilman who played for a national championship team at the University of Arkansas. Jones loved football and wanted to be part of the NFL.

So Jones bought the Dallas Cowboys for $140 million. One of the first things Jones did was replace Tom Landry, the only coach the Cowboys ever had. Landry had a 270–178–6

Dallas Cowboys coach Jimmy Johnson, *left*, and owner Jerry Jones brought the Cowboys dynasty back.

Troy Aikman drops back to pass against the Oakland Raiders during the 1996 preseason.

record and had won two Super Bowls with Dallas, where he had

become a legend.

Jones hired his former college teammate at the

University of Arkansas, Jimmy Johnson. Johnson had been a

successful college coach at Oklahoma State University and Miami of Florida. The Cowboys set about retooling a roster that had grown stale and had won only 17 games over the previous three seasons.

In 1989, their first year together, the Cowboys went 1–15, the worst record in the NFL. But better days would be coming.

BUILDING THROUGH THE DRAFT

Before Jones and Johnson arrived, the Cowboys took receiver Michael Irvin in the 1988 draft. Dallas drafted quarterback Troy Aikman of UCLA first overall in 1989. Then the Cowboys made a move that would pay off for years to come. Johnson decided the quickest way to rebuild the roster was to trade his best player, Herschel Walker. The Minnesota Vikings believed the star running back was just what they needed to win a championship. So the two teams worked out one of the biggest deals in football history.

The Cowboys wound up with five players, but even more important, they got eight draft picks over four years from Minnesota. Among the players they selected with those picks were running back Emmitt Smith, wide receiver Alvin Harper, and safety Darren Woodson, all of whom became stars of the 1990s dynasty.

Many NFL teams believed coaches from college football couldn't win in the pros. But by 1991, Johnson was ready to prove otherwise. He'd built a roster of strong, young, fast, energetic players. He convinced them that the rest of the NFL thought they weren't good enough.

In 1991 the Cowboys were good enough to make the playoffs at 11–5, and they beat the Chicago Bears before losing to the Detroit Lions. Led by "the Triplets"—Aikman, Smith, and Irvin—they won 13 games the next season. That was second only to the San Francisco 49ers' 14 wins.

Smith was first-team All-Pro, and Irvin made second team. It was the first of six brilliant years together for the Triplets. But were they ready for a championship?

After beating the Philadelphia Eagles 34–10 in the first round of the playoffs, they would find out in San Francisco. The 49ers had won four Super Bowls in nine seasons. They were the home team and had the experience Dallas did not.

The Cowboys didn't care. Tied 10–10 at halftime, Johnson told his players that the 49ers were ready to be beaten. Aikman completed 70 percent of his passes for 322 yards and two touchdowns. Smith had two touchdowns and 114 yards rushing. Their defense had three sacks and two interceptions of league Most Valuable Player (MVP) and future Hall of Fame quarterback Steve Young. As they celebrated on the sideline

THE HERSCHEL WALKER TRADE

In the Herschel Walker trade, Dallas sent Walker, two third-round draft picks, a fifth-rounder, and a 10th-rounder to Minnesota. It got back Minnesota's first-, second-, and fifth-round picks in the 1990 draft. The Cowboys also got five players in the trade. Each player had a conditional draft pick assigned to him, and the Cowboys could choose to keep the player or take the pick after the season ended. Johnson cut all of the players who had arrived in the trade. Dallas ended up with eight of Minnesota's draft choices in the trade Johnson referred to as "The Great Train Robbery."

with high fives and hugs, the Cowboys understood what they'd done. Next stop: the Super Bowl.

CHAPTER 4

THE LOMBARDI
TROPHIES

T o become a dynasty, a team must win a few championships over a span of years. When the Cowboys took on the Buffalo Bills for the 1992 NFL title, they hadn't ridden off with a Lombardi Trophy since the 1977 season.

The Bills were in the midst of their own dynasty of sorts. This would be their third straight appearance in a Super Bowl. Only the 1971–73 Miami Dolphins had gotten to three in a row. But Buffalo had been beaten by the

Troy Aikman scrambles away from a defender during Super Bowl XXVII.

Emmitt Smith shakes off two New York Giants defenders.

New York Giants and Washington Redskins in the previous two Super Bowls. Now they faced another NFC East power in Dallas.

The Cowboys were a seven-point favorite at the Rose Bowl in California, even though the team was young, and the Bills had been down this road two straight years.

The Bills scored first for a 7–0 lead. That was the only time they smiled all day. By halftime Aikman had thrown for three touchdowns, two to Michael Irvin, and Dallas was ahead 28–10.

Buffalo closed to 31–17 before the Cowboys scored three more times, including another toss by Aikman, the game's MVP.

The 52–17 victory was the second-biggest rout in Super Bowl history at the time. Jimmy Johnson didn't even mind when his players messed up his famously arranged hairdo. "Winning is all I care about," Johnson said, pumping his fists.

COWBOYS REPEAT

With a championship in their pockets and a young, talented roster, the Cowboys were heavy favorites to repeat in 1993. But then they had a problem in training camp. Star running back Emmitt Smith, who had led the NFL in rushing in 1991 and 1992, was unhappy with his contract. Smith sat out training camp, and his protest dragged into the regular season.

Dallas lost its first two games, and team owner Jerry Jones quickly gave Smith a new contract. Smith repaid Jones by becoming league MVP, again leading the NFL in rushing, and helping Dallas recover by winning seven straight games.

But before the Cowboys could think Super Bowl, they had to play the final regular-season game at the New York Giants.

The winner would claim the NFC East title and a playoff bye. The loser would have to settle for a wild-card spot in the playoffs.

Smith rushed for 168 yards and caught 10 passes for 61 yards even though he had a separated right shoulder. Every time he hit the frozen turf, he was in pain. Aikman passed for 180 yards and Dallas's only touchdown. He completed 80 percent of his passes in the freezing cold. Together Aikman and Smith hung in and helped Dallas win 16–13 in overtime.

Smith had a week off to heal, and Dallas then beat the Green Bay Packers and San Francisco 49ers in the playoffs. Now the Cowboys could think about the Super Bowl.

A familiar foe was waiting for them in Atlanta, the site of the big game. Buffalo had become the first and only team to make four straight Super Bowls. The Bills also became the only team to lose four in a row as Dallas thumped them 30–13. The game was close for a while, with Buffalo on top 13–6 at halftime. But James Washington returned a fumble 48 yards early in the second half for a tying touchdown. Aikman had a rough game, with no passing touchdowns and an interception. But then Smith took charge, rushing for two touchdowns, and the

Emmitt Smith rushes for 132 yards and Super Bowl MVP honors in 1994.

second Dallas dynasty was secured. Smith added a Super Bowl MVP trophy to his regular-season award.

"Our mission is completed," Smith said. "We came into this season with the idea of doing this. It's been a super year for me as well as my teammates. Being MVP of the league and this game, you can't ask for anything more."

CHAPTER 5

AFTERMATH

I n 1995 the Dallas Cowboys became the second team with five Lombardi Trophies. But through 2017, America's Team hadn't even been back to the Super Bowl, let alone win another one. What happened?

Lots of things, starting with owner Jerry Jones replacing coaches. After he fired Barry Switzer, who coached the Super Bowl-winning 1995 Cowboys, Jones went through a string of largely unsuccessful coaches. Chan Gailey,

Jerry Jones receives the Lombardi Trophy after Super Bowl XXX.

Dave Campo, Bill Parcells, and Wade Phillips combined to go 102–105 from 1998 to midway through the 2010 season.

Thankfully for Dallas fans, Jones seemed to find the right coach when he replaced Phillips with Jason Garrett halfway through the 2010 schedule. Garrett helped turn around the Cowboys, who had only one losing record in his first seven full seasons at the helm. They won two NFC East crowns in that span.

Changing coaches is one thing. Losing great players is another. Soon after the three Super Bowl wins in four years, four of Dallas's future Hall of Famers began to lose their edge.

Aikman, the greatest passer in Cowboys history, retired in 2000. Aikman says he suffered seven or eight concussions in his professional career. After winning his third Super Bowl in four years, Aikman's play—and the play of those around him— declined quickly. His record as a starter was 34–33 over his final five seasons. In 2006 Aikman was inducted into the Hall of Fame in Canton, Ohio. He called the 1994 Super Bowl win his greatest on-field accomplishments.

"I have a real hard time classifying anything as my biggest moment, my favorite color or whatever," Aikman said. "I'd have

Troy Aikman was a six-time Pro Bowl quarterback during his 12-year career at Dallas.

to say, though, that the Super Bowl was my greatest moment in sports, and it was also my most emotional moment."

Emmitt Smith had more good years in him after the Cowboys' last Super Bowl than did his quarterback. He rushed for at least 1,000 yards six more times and had 975 yards in his final season with Dallas. Smith then joined the Arizona Cardinals in 2002 and retired after 2004 as the NFL's career rushing leader with 18,355 yards. Smith entered the Hall of Fame in 2010.

Michael Irvin remained "the Playmaker" for the Cowboys through 1998. But he barely played in 1999 before retiring. A year after Aikman entered the Hall of Fame, Irvin did too.

Jimmy Johnson didn't stop coaching when he left Dallas. He also had very little success when he joined the Miami Dolphins. As he did in Dallas when he replaced Tom Landry, Johnson followed a coaching legend in Miami: Don Shula, the winningest coach in NFL history. But Johnson didn't win a Super Bowl in Miami, and his teams went 38–31 with a 1–3 playoff mark.

JERRY JONES

Jerry Jones also is general manager of the Cowboys and since 1989 has had final call on their draft picks. He hit the jackpot in 2016 with two of his selections. First-round pick Ezekiel Elliott, a running back from Ohio State, led the NFL in rushing as a rookie. In the fourth round, Dallas took quarterback Dak Prescott from Mississippi State. All he did was win the Offensive Rookie of the Year Award. Prescott and Elliot won 13 games as rookies and won their division as rookies.

The Dallas Cowboys now play in AT&T Stadium in Arlington, Texas.

A LASTING LEGACY

Things got pretty rough for the Cowboys from 2000 to 2005. They appeared in just one playoff game, a wild-card loss at Carolina. In fact they went from 1997 through 2008 without a postseason victory. But they remained one of the most popular franchises in all of sports. By 2017 they were worth $4 billion. That is more than any other team in any other sport.

AT&T Stadium in Arlington, Texas, opened to much fanfare in 2009. The Cowboys' new home is considered almost space-age. Major events in other sports take place there every year. Through the years since the Cowboys dynasty, fans still love to watch their team play in person or on TV.

TEAM FILE

DALLAS COWBOYS

SPAN OF DYNASTY

- 1991–92 through 1994–95

SUPER BOWLS WON

- 3 (1992, 1993, 1995)

NFC EAST TITLES WON

- 4 (1992, 1993, 1994, 1995)

REGULAR-SEASON RECORD

- 49–15

PLAYOFFS RECORD

- 10–1

KEY RIVALS

- Buffalo Bills
- Green Bay Packers
- New York Giants
- Pittsburgh Steelers
- San Francisco 49ers

INDIVIDUAL AWARDS

NFL MVP

- Emmitt Smith (1993)

SUPER BOWL MVP

- Troy Aikman (1992)
- Emmitt Smith (1993)
- Larry Brown (1995)

NFL OFFENSIVE ROOKIE OF THE YEAR

- Emmitt Smith (1990)

COACH OF THE YEAR

- Jimmy Johnson (1990)

PRO FOOTBALL HALL OF FAME

- Troy Aikman (2006)
- Michael Irvin (2007)
- Emmitt Smith (2010)
- Jerry Jones (2017)

JANUARY 28, 1960

The Cowboys are granted an NFL expansion franchise.

JANUARY 1, 1967

Dallas makes its first playoff, but loses to Green Bay.

DECEMBER 31, 1967

Dallas loses the "Ice Bowl" at Green Bay on the final play as the Packers win the NFL crown 21–17.

JANUARY 17, 1971

After the fifth straight playoff appearance, the Cowboys make the Super Bowl but lose to Baltimore 16–13.

JANUARY 16, 1972

Led by Roger Staubach, Dallas beats Miami 24–3 for the 1971 Super Bowl.

JANUARY 15, 1978

Landry and Staubach lead the Cowboys to the 1977 Super Bowl, beating Denver 27–10.

FEBRUARY 25, 1989

Jerry Jones buys the team.

APRIL 22, 1990

Dallas drafts Emmitt Smith.

JANUARY 31, 1993

The Cowboys get back to the Super Bowl and defeat Buffalo 52–17.

JANUARY 30, 1994

For the first time, Dallas repeats as champion, beating the Bills again, 30–13.

MARCH 29, 1994

Johnson quits as coach. Jones hires Barry Switzer.

JANUARY 28, 1996

In the final Super Bowl trip for the Triplets, the Cowboys beat the Steelers 27–17 in the Super Bowl.

BYE
A week during the season that a team does not have a game.

DRAFT
A system that allows teams to acquire new players coming into a league.

DYNASTY
A team that has an extended period of success, usually winning multiple championships in the process.

FRANCHISE
A sports organization, including the top-level team and all its minor league affiliates.

HALL OF FAME
An honor given to the very best participants in a sport.

OVERTIME
An extra period of play when the score is tied after regulation.

PLAYOFFS
A set of games played after the regular season that decide which team is the champion.

QUARTERBACK
The player who calls plays and throws passes.

RIVAL
An opponent with whom a player or team has a fierce and ongoing competition.

ROSTER
A list of players that make up a team.

ONLINE RESOURCES

Booklinks
NONFICTION NETWORK
FREE! ONLINE NONFICTION RESOURCES

To learn more about Troy Aikman and the Dallas Cowboys, visit abdobooklinks.com.
These links are routinely monitored and updated to provide the most current
information available.

BOOKS

Glave, Tom. *Dallas Cowboys*. Minneapolis: Abdo, 2017.

Martin, Brett S. *STEM in Football*. Minneapolis: Abdo, 2018.

Wilner, Barry. *Total Football*. Minneapolis: Abdo, 2017.

MORE INFORMATION

ABOUT THE AUTHOR

Barry Wilner has been a sportswriter for The Associated Press since 1976 and has covered the Super Bowl, Olympics, World Cup, Stanley Cup Finals, and many other major sports events. He has written more than 60 books. Barry lives in Garnerville, New York.